Dreaming of Tomorrow

Julia Nagler

BookLeaf Publishing

Presentation by *BookLeaf Publishing*

Web: www.bookleafpub.com

E-mail: info@bookleafpub.com

ISBN: 9789357441452

First edition 2023

DEDICATION

To the teacher who said "someday you'll all be reading her stories," and my pen-pal who told me about inspiring female authors

Who Are You

"Who are you?"
I get asked this on the first day of every school year
And each time my answer changes
But it's not because I change
I just don't know
I guess it depends on who I'm with
With some I'm an open book
With others a locked treasure chest
With some I'm energetic
With others stoic
Or maybe its just how they see me
Some see me as a hero
Others a villain
Some see me as smart
Others not
I've been called
"Overly-apolegetic"
"Excited easily"
"Talkative"
And "Quiet"
Maybe it depends on my day
When I'm having a good day, I'm nice
And the reverse
I hope I have the answer one day
I can't wait to meet me
Whoever I am
Whoever I become
I hope I make someone happy
I hope I make me happy

Missing You

Some people leave
for a week
a month
a year
but when you leave
for even a day
it feels like forever
and now you're gone
for real
forever
so until I see you again
somewhere among the stars
remember me
and I'll remember you

Imperfect

I'm imperfect
Everyone is, but I dont notice
When you only see someone every once in awhile,
You notice the things you like
Their smile
Their eyes
Their hair
You dont see them long enough to notice
The flaws
Maybe they have crooked teeth
Or frizzy hair
But you see yourself so often
You do notice
Every
Little
Flaw
You might be the only one who notices your
Cracked lips
Or little pimples
I notice these things
But only about myself
I look to close in the mirror
I see the things that are the last things anyone else sees

But I notice
I try to fix everything
I brush my hair a million times
I apply chapstick
I see another girl and see perfection
I know she sees something else
So don’t look to hard in the mirror
I think you're perfect

The four seasons

Summer is first
the world is filled with green
the sun warms the earth
summer storms freshen the grass
then fall comes
beginning to kill off the beauty of summer
cold wind begins to chill the earth
until the world is asleep
and winter comes
the smell of cold air makes the cold almost
enjoyable
and the stars are prettiest because
the world sleeps
resting and readying to grow again
when spring comes
green and all the color of the world return
dandelions turn from yellow to white
tulips sprout
then summer returns

Fireflies

light up the summer night,
glowing bright throughout their flight,
catch a few in a jar,
it's like catching a star
constellations on the ground
that's where they'll be found
where are they during the day?
where do they stray?
I might never know
could I follow their glow?
but they reappear every night
with their bright light
couldn't count them if I try
like grains of sand or stars in the sky

Wishes

I used to wish on everything
throwing pennies into a fountain
blowing eyelashes and dandelions
shooting stars
and ladybugs
I wished to grow up
I wished to have a good day
I wished for silly things
now it seems I only wish for one thing
to go back in time
to when I still believed in wishes

Well Behaved Women

Lauren Thatcher once said
"well behaved women seldom make history"
historians say the meaning of this
is you have to be extrodinairy
you have do do great things to make change
to be noticed
but what if instead
she was praising
the mothers raising the future of our world
the wives being inspirations for poets and artists
all these people behind the scenes
she is saying that these important women aren't
celebrated and praised for their help
she is thanking all the women who came before her
and all the women to come
whether recognized or not
so thank you
to the mothers
and grandmothers
and wives
raising and inspiring our future

Pictures

The beauty of life is so great
you can't always find it in a photograph
you can't capture the jokes
or the friends
or the song of birds
when you hide behind a camera lens
you miss what's right in front of you
your phone can't capture the full beauty
you have to be there
experience the moment that an image can't show
no matter the size of your lens

Sleepless Nights

Don't you hate it
when you can’t turn your mind off
the gears keep turning
sleep doesn't come

when you lay in bed for hours
but cant close your eyes for more than five
minutes
your eyes hurt
and you feel insanely tired

when you know your not
nervous
or excited

when you shouldn't be awake
but you can't fall asleep

it feels as though,
you’re the only person in the world
silent
dark
and a bit creepy

and eventually
you give up on sleep
you watch a show
or read a book
until everybody else awakes
and that's when finally,
you fall asleep.

Permanent

Nothing is permanent
everyone leaves eventually
the seasons change
stars die
and new plants grow
I knew you would leave eventually
I didn't know how though
and I didn't know it would hurt so much
because for a second I forgot
that eventually
you would disapear from my life
but you will never disappear from my memories

Quiet

Apparently,
I'm quiet
I've never noticed
it's so loud
in my head
in my heart
voices yelling
that I have to be
perfect
strong
polite
how can they think I'm quiet
when it feels so loud

Sticky Stars

You know those glowing
sticky stars
I loved them when I was little
I stuck about a million to my ceiling
they warded of the darkness
which to a 5 year old was
pretty damn scary.
they made the night not so
terrifying.
I thought that the little light
Would get rid of the monsters

But then my stars
They started falling
One by one they lost their cling
And fell to the floor
So I started catching them
And putting them back
But every day more fell
Faster and faster

The other day I realized
I can't catch the stars
I can't ward off the darkness
Or the monsters in it
So I gave up
And all my stars fell

Tides

In the ocean
when you are toppled by waves and tides
you are told not to struggle
it only gives the rough waves more control
everytime you stand up
everytime you take a breath
another wave comes
knocking you back to the seafloor

Morning

my favorite part of the day,
is the beginning
I wake before the sun does
before my family
the quiet is beautiful
my head is clear
I shower
hot water waking every part of me
I crack my spine
twisting and cracking like a glowstick
once the sun is awake
everyone else is too
the world gets loud
I have things to do
the chaos ensues
then by the end
the peace has come back
the sun has fallen asleep
and I do to
before my day begins again

Years

Time passes in an odd way
time goes faster as you grow
some days go by like they never existed
and others never seem to end
I'm growing up too quickly
I wish I was a kid
yet when I was a kid
I wished to grow up
life as begun to move to fast
I'm worried I can't stop the passage
I watch the clock for a minute and years have passed
I hadn't even noticed they were there

Hopefully you miss me

Hopefully you miss me
as much as I do you
I want you to be happy
but not with her
with me
hopefully you're as broken as me
maybe you hurting to
will lessen my hurt
hopefully you remember me
as your first love
as your first kiss
as your old best friend
hopefully you miss me
because I worry
I'll never stop missing you

Birds

I love watching birds fly
they take leaps
trusting that they can catch themselves
I don't know how they do it
I can't
I can't take the jump
I can't take the risk
what if my wings let me down
what if I don't soar
what if I fall
what if I made a mistake?
I hope I can take the leap

Butterflies

I hate the butterflies
that live in my stomach
they seem to flutter constantly
but they go away when you're around
you scare them away
with your intoxicating laugh
and contagious smile
I wish you were with me all the time
then they would never be there

memories

Memories,
they fill my mind
influencing me
changing me
teaching me.
people I have known
things they have said
pain they have inflicted
Memories,
they fill my mind
influencing me
changing me
teaching me.
the worst of my sadness
the happiest of my joys
the best of people
Memories,
they fill my mind
influencing me
changing me
teaching me.
adventures I have had
the craziness of life
the ups and downs
Memories,
they fill my mind
influencing me
changing me

teaching me.
things I have done
things I wish I could take back
things I would do a thousand times over
Memories,
they fill my mind
influencing me
changing me
teaching me.
some I hate to think of
some I never want to stop
Memories,
they fill my mind
influencing me
changing me
teaching me.
Memories of
joy and sadness
calmness and fear
hope and faith
people and words
places and journeys
Memories,
they fill my mind
influencing me
changing me
teaching me.
they make me who I am
so even the worst ones,
I wouldn't trade for anything

Storm

Life is a storm
constant changing
some days you can hide in the eye
and all is well
others can be a storm of tears
flooding your mind
and you feel like you might drown
some days a tornado appears in your lungs
forcing the air out
some days an earthquake shakes you to your core
but on those few days
where you're in the eye of it all
breeze fills your lungs again
the ground is stable
and everything feels okay
even if for just a moment

www.ingramcontent.com/pod-product-compliance
Lightning Source LLC
Chambersburg PA
CBHW051719130826
49812CB00034B/1261
* 9 7 8 9 3 5 7 4 4 1 4 5 2 *